BLACK MILLIONAIRES OF TOMORROW

A Wealth-Building Study Guide for Children
Grade 4 - 5

STOCKS

by Dr. Boyce Watkins

TABLE OF CONTENTS

Letter from Dr. Boyce Watkins iii

Introduction to Stocks 2

Stocks 3

Stock Market 6

Stockbroker 9

Stock Exchange 12

Stock Prices 16

Bulls and Bears 19

Dividends 22

Mutual Funds 25

Stock Market Myths 28

Answer Key 31

About the Author 38

Letter from Dr. Boyce Watkins

Dear Middle Schoolers,

As you think about the phrase *financial literacy*, I want you to explore all of the various ways that you come in contact with money. Perhaps you do chores around the house and receive an allowance. Or, maybe, you earn money by babysitting or by doing lawn care.

It is important that you understand what money is, its value, and how to save and invest for your future. That's right; it is not too early for you to think about your financial future. In fact, as a pre-teen, this is the best time to start engaging in habits that will carry you through middle school, high school, and beyond.

This book is designed to help your teachers, math specialists, and parents teach you about financial literacy and wealth building.

In each lesson, you will engage in different learning activities. Each one will help you think about how you can apply financial literacy skills to your everyday life.

I know that you are capable of being great, and it all starts with the decisions that you make today!

Dr. Boyce Watkins

An Introduction to Stocks

Welcome to the Black Millionaires of Tomorrow lesson on stocks. Created by Dr. Boyce Watkins, this lesson will prepare you as a future shareholder. You will learn about the stock market, the benefits/risks of investing in stocks, and much more. By the end of this lesson, you will understand how the stock market works and how you can invest in it.

LEARNING STANDARDS:
This lesson is aligned to the Common Core State Standards for learning. Students will learn and practice concepts in the areas of Reading, Writing and Mathematics.

LEARNING GOAL:
Students will learn how to obtain wealth and financial security through stock investments.

Stocks Pre-Lesson KWL Chart

The K-W-L chart helps you to think about your personal learning goals before you begin a lesson. What do you already know about stocks? What do you want to know? After the lesson is completed, come back to this chart and reflect on what you have learned.

Complete the chart by listing what you know, want to know, and have learned (after the lesson) about stocks.
Know
Want to know
Learned

Stocks

Words That Matter
Find these words in the lesson!

stock	a part or share of a company's ownership
share	a unit of ownership
shareholders	a person who owns shares in a company

COMMON CORE STATE STANDARDS
- CCRA.L.2
  Demonstrate command of the conventions of standard English capitalization, punctuation, and spelling when writing.
- CCSS.ELA-LITERACY.W.4.4-W.6.4
  Produce clear and coherent writing in which the development and organization are appropriate to task, purpose, and audience.
- CCSS.MATH.CONTENT.4.NF.B.4.C
  Solve word problems involving multiplication of a fraction by a whole number
- CCSS.MATH.CONTENT.4.NBT.B.4 & 5 - Fluently add, subtract and multiply multi-digit whole numbers using the standard algorithm

LEARNING GOAL:
Students will gain a basic understanding of stocks.

❓ Question to Ponder:

Why do companies sell stocks?
_____
_____
_____
_____

Let's Explore the Topic:
Think about the concept of sharing. You own something, like a bag of snacks, but you give each of your friends a portion from that bag. Businesses offer **stocks** to investors who want to buy a portion of the company. These investors purchase **shares** and are now partial owners. The company and its **shareholders** both benefit from the deal. Shareholders gain ownership (and the chance to make more money), while companies use cash from stock purchases to run their business.

Extension Activity
Search the internet for "Top 10 Stocks to Buy." You may see your favorite department store or cell phone company on the list. Why do you think people want to own parts of these companies?

Digging Deeper: Understanding Stock

The Burger Shop

The Burger Shop is a privately owned company. Currently, Ken Washington owns 3 locations of The Burger Shop. He wants to build more locations, but he cannot afford it. Ken decides to offer stock in his company so that he can raise more money.

Ken finds 3 investors who would like to buy stock in The Burger Shop. Read about each investor and use mathematics to calculate the total investment.

Example: Harold wants to purchase 85 shares at $53.28 each. Calculate the total cost of Harold's investment.

$$85 \times \$53.28 = \$4,528.80$$

Harold will invest a total $4,528.80

Investor 1: Jaheim wants to purchase 50 shares priced at $16.08 each. Calculate the total cost of Jaheim's investment.

Investor 2: Brandy wants to purchase 75 shares priced at $16.08 each. Calculate the total cost of Brandy's investment.

Investor 3: Vincent wants to purchase 120 shares priced at $16.08 each. He plans to later sell ¾ of his stocks at a higher price. Calculate the total cost of Vincent's investment. How many shares does he plan to sell?

Stocks Lesson Review

1. Why would a company want to sell portions of its ownership?
   _____
   _____
   _____
   _____
   _____

2. Which of the following is a term describing someone who owns stocks?
   a) Share
   b) Stockbroker
   c) Shareholders
   d) Stock market

3. Think of a company that you might want to invest in. Why would you like to purchase stock from this company?
   _____
   _____
   _____
   _____
   _____

Stock Market Pre-Lesson KWL Chart

The K-W-L chart helps you to think about your personal learning goals before you begin a lesson. What do you already know about the stock market? What do you want to know? After the lesson is completed, come back to this chart and reflect on what you have learned.

Complete the chart by listing what you know, want to know, and have learned (after the lesson) about the stock market.

Know

Want to know

Learned

Stock Market

Words That Matter
Find these words in the lesson!

stock market	a place where people buy and sell stock
trade	to buy and sell stock
Securities and Exchange Commission (SEC)	an agency that oversees the stock market in order to promote fairness and prevent fraud.

COMMON CORE STATE STANDARDS
- CCRA.L.2
  Demonstrate command of the conventions of standard English capitalization, punctuation, and spelling when writing.
- CCSS.ELA-LITERACY.W.4.4-W.6.4
  Produce clear and coherent writing in which the development and organization are appropriate to task, purpose, and audience.

LEARNING GOAL:
Students will be able to explain how the stock market works.

Question to Ponder:

What is the stock market and how does it work?
_____
_____
_____
_____

Let's Explore the Topic:

The **stock market** is not an actual store like the market you buy your food from. The term stock market can refer a physical location or a virtual platform. People can **trade** stocks through an exchange (you will learn more about this in the next section) such as the NYSE, or an online market like E*TRADE.

There are many laws to make sure that people are treated fairly on the stock market. Companies and investors cannot easily steal or lie about money. **The Securities and Exchange Commission** makes sure that your money is safe.

 ## Extension Activity

Watch a newscast with your parents. Listen for news about the stock market. What is going on? Is it good news or bad news? Which companies are the news reporters talking about?

 ## Digging Deeper: Getting Started on the Market

Do Your Research

One of the first steps to buying stock is researching your options. Suppose that you were thinking about buying stocks online. You are planning to invest $500. Look at the information below and explain which option you would choose.

Ally Invest	Vanguard	Charles Schwab	E*TRADE	Fidelity
✓ $4.95 per trade	✓ $7.00 per trade	✓ $4.95 per trade	✓ $6.95 per trade	✓ $4.95 per trade
✓ $0 Minimum Investment	✓ $3,000 Minimum Investment	✓ $1,000 Minimum Investment	✓ $500 Minimum Investment	✓ $2,500 Minimum Investment

Write a paragraph explaining which option you would choose and why.

Stock Market Lesson Review

1. Describe at least one way that you can buy stock.
   _____
   _____
   _____
   _____
   _____

2. Which of the following best describes the stock market?
   a) A supermarket where people go to buy stocks
   b) A physical or virtual market where people buy stocks
   c) A person who sells stocks
   d) A company that owns stocks

Stockbroker Pre-Lesson KWL Chart

The K-W-L chart helps you to think about your personal learning goals before you begin a lesson. What do you already know about the stockbrokers? What do you want to know? After the lesson is completed, come back to this chart and reflect on what you have learned.

Complete the chart by listing what you know, want to know, and have learned (after the lesson) about the stockbrokers.

Know

Want to know

Learned

Black Millionaires of Tomorrow

Stockbroker

Words That Matter
Find these words in the lesson!

stockbroker	a professional who buys and sells stocks on behalf of an investor
intermediary	a person who acts as a middleman/woman between two participants in a financial deal
broker fees	a fee charged to an investor in exchange for broker services
brokerage	a company or service acting as a stockbroker

COMMON CORE STATE STANDARDS
- CCRA.L.2 - Demonstrate command of the conventions of standard English capitalization, punctuation, and spelling when writing.
- CCSS.ELA-LITERACY.W.4.4-W.6.4 - Produce clear and coherent writing in which the development and organization are appropriate to task, purpose, and audience.
- CCSS.MATH.CONTENT.4.NBT.B.4 & 5
  Fluently add, subtract and multiply multi-digit whole numbers using the standard algorithm
- CCSS.MATH.CONTENT.6.RP.A.3.C- Find a percent of a quantity as a rate per 100

LEARNING GOAL:
Students will be able to describe the role and responsibilities of a stockbroker.

❓ Question to Ponder:

What do stockbrokers do? How do they help investors?
_____
_____
_____
_____

Let's Explore the Topic:

The stock market is not like an ordinary market. When you want something from the store, you can go get it yourself. But if you want to buy stocks, you will need some type of **intermediary**. The intermediary is the one who will manage the trade. This could be a **stockbroker** or an online **brokerage**. As an investor, you have the luxury of hiring special professionals to do your "shopping" for you!

Stockbrokers can also advise and manage your investments. They can be extremely helpful as you begin investing in the stock market. These services are not free, however. **Broker fees** could be just a few dollars per trade, or a small percentage of your total investments.

 ### Extension Activity

Visit a local brokerage in your community. Learn about what a stockbroker does and how their services are valuable to the community.

 ## Digging Deeper: Stockbrokers

The Famous Stockbroker

Christopher Gardner is a well-known African-American stockbroker. He earned wealth by investing in the stock market and running his own brokerage in Chicago, Illinois.

Pretend that you have hired Mr. Gardner to help you buy stocks. Look at the scenarios below and use mathematics to answer the questions.

Example: Mr. Gardner charges you $9.95 per trade. You purchase 30 shares for $43.17 each. What is the total cost of your investment?

$$30 \times \$43.17 = \$1,294.20$$
$$\$1,294.20 + \$9.95 \text{ fee} = \$1,304.15$$
Total Cost = $1,304.15

Mr. Gardner's broker fee is 2% of your total investments. You purchase 100 shares at $163.22 each. How much money will you owe Mr. Gardner for his services?

A local competitor, Jada Morris, offers her brokerage services for $6.95 per trade (or per share purchase). If you conduct the same deal as the scenario above, whose services will cost you more? Mr. Gardner or Mrs. Morris?

Stock Broker Lesson Review

1. Explain what a stock broker does and how he/she can help you buy stock.
   _____
   _____
   _____
   _____
   _____

2. Which of these terms define a stockbroker's role?
   a) intermediary
   b) advisor
   c) investment manager
   d) all of the above

3. Why do you think stockbrokers charge a fee for their services?
   _____
   _____
   _____
   _____
   _____

Stock Exchange Pre-Lesson KWL Chart

The K-W-L chart helps you to think about your personal learning goals before you begin a lesson. What do you already know about the stock exchange? What do you want to know? After the lesson is completed, come back to this chart and reflect on what you have learned.

Complete the chart by listing what you know, want to know, and have learned (after the lesson) about the stock exchange.

Know

Want to know

Learned

The Stock Exchange

Words That Matter
Find these words in the lesson!

stock exchange	a worldwide market in which stocks are bought and sold
New York Stock Exchange (NYSE)	the largest stock exchange in the world
National Association of Securities Dealers Automated Quotations (NASDAQ)	the second-largest stock exchange in the world
foreign investments	investments made in a company that is based in a another country
listed	appears on a stock exchange list of companies for public trading

COMMON CORE STATE STANDARDS
- CCRA.L.2 - Demonstrate command of the conventions of standard English capitalization, punctuation, and spelling when writing.
- CCSS.ELA-LITERACY.W.4.4-W.6.4 - Produce clear and coherent writing in which the development and organization are appropriate to task, purpose, and audience.

LEARNING GOAL:
Students will learn about the purpose and function of the stock exchange.

? Question to Ponder:

How can investors buy stocks from companies all over the world?
_____
_____
_____
_____

Let's Explore the Topic:

The stock exchange is where buyers and sellers come together to make trades. There are stock exchanges are over the world. The two largest stock exchanges, NYSE and NASDAQ, are located in the United States. There are also major stock exchanges in England, Japan and India. Your stockbroker can help you make foreign investments with companies overseas. However, the company must be listed in order for you to purchase shares.

Extension Activity

The New York Stock Exchange on Wall Street is a popular tourist spot. Research what happens at the New York Stock Exchange building. What would you like to observe if you had a chance to visit the NYSE?

Digging Deeper: Stocks around the World

Top 10 Stock Exchanges

Look at the chart below. These are the top 10 stocks exchanges in the world. Read the scenarios and decide which exchange applies to the stock purchase.

Example: Bryant wants to purchase stock in a company based in Tokyo. Which exchange would this company be listed on?
The company would be listed on the Shanghai Stock Exchange, which is based in Tokyo.

Rank	Exchange	Economy	Headquarters
1	New York Stock Exchange	United States	New York
2	NASDAQ	United States	New York
3	Japan Exchange Group	Japan	Tokyo
4	Shanghai Stock Exchange	China	Shanghai
5	Euronext	European Union	Amsterdam Brussels Lisbon London Paris
6	London Stock Exchange	United Kingdom	London
7	Hong Kong Stock Exchange	Hong Kong	Hong Kong
8	Shenzhen Stock Exchange	China	Shenzhen
9	TMX Group	Canada	Toronto
10	National Stock Exchange of India	India	Mumbai

Mario wants to purchase stock in Maple Leaf Manufacturing, a company based in Canada. Which stock exchange would this company be listed on?

LaToya wants to purchase stock in Beauté Noire Cosmetics, a company based in Paris, France. Which stock exchange would this company be listed on?

Ronnie wants to purchase stock in Nintendo, a company based in Japan. Which stock exchange would this company be listed on?

Taj wants to purchase stock in Rajesh Exports, a company based in India. Which stock exchange would this company be listed on?

Mario wants to purchase stock in Mattel, a company based in California. Which stock exchange (or exchanges) would this company be listed on?

Stock Exchange Lesson Review

1. Explain how investors can purchase stock in foreign countries.
   _____
   _____
   _____
   _____

2. Which of the following is true about stock exchanges? Select **ALL** that apply.
   a) There is only 1 stock exchange in the world.
   b) There are many stock exchanges all over the world.
   c) The largest stock exchange is located in the United States.
   d) The second largest stock exchange is located in Japan.
   e) The stock exchange is where buyers and sellers come together to make trades.

Stock Prices Pre-Lesson KWL Chart

The K-W-L chart helps you to think about your personal learning goals before you begin a lesson. What do you already know about the stock prices? What do you want to know? After the lesson is completed, come back to this chart and reflect on what you have learned.

Complete the chart by listing what you know, want to know, and have learned (after the lesson) about the stock prices.

Know

Want to know

Learned

Black Millionaires of Tomorrow

Stock Prices

Words That Matter
Find these words in the lesson!

stock price	the cost of a single share
volatility	the likelihood of a stock price changing over time
supply and demand	the availability of shares vs. the amount of people who want to buy them
ticker symbol	an abbreviation that represents a specific company
change direction	an symbol that points upward/downward to indicate a rise or fall in a stock price
change amount	The difference in a stock price compared to the previous day

COMMON CORE STATE STANDARDS
- CCRA.L.2 - Demonstrate command of the conventions of standard English capitalization, punctuation, and spelling when writing.
- CCSS.ELA-LITERACY.W.4.4-W.6.4 - Produce clear and coherent writing in which the development and organization are appropriate to task, purpose, and audience.

LEARNING GOAL:
Students will learn about stock prices and explore the reasons why they might change.

? Question to Ponder:

Why do stock prices change?
_____
_____
_____
_____

16

Black Millionaires of Tomorrow

🔍 Let's Explore the Topic:

Each share that you purchase has a specific value. However, that value will change over time. **Stock prices** rise and fall constantly, although some stocks have a higher **volatility** than others. This is due to factors such as **supply and demand**. If more investors are selling a particular stock than buying it, the price will fall. Companies who have more potential buyers tend to have higher stock prices. Stock prices also change based on the economy and overall market.

Have you ever seen those odd-looking numbers and symbols floating across the bottom of your TV screen? This information tells people about stock prices. Look at the example below:

The **ticker symbol** MSFT is short for the company Microsoft. Notice how Microsoft's stock prices are changing in this example. The **change direction** arrow is pointing downward. This means that the price has fallen. The **change amount** shows how much the price has dropped. Price drops are usually shown in red text, while a rise is shown in green.

Extension Activity

Select a company's stock and check on it daily for a week. How did the prices change? Why do you think this happened?
Suggested websites: marketwatch.com and money.cnn.com
You can also check on stocks by watching news reports.

Digging Deeper: Track your stocks

Stock Price Changes

Look at the information for each company and explain how the prices have changed.

Example: Mattel Inc. Stock Prices
MAT ▲ + 3.80

Explanation: Mattel's stock prices have increased. The arrow is pointing upward, and the positive green number indicates a price rise.

Apple Inc AAPL ▼ - 2.41	Explanation:
Sony Corp SNE ▼ - 0.90	Explanation:
Walt Disney Co DIS ▲ + 0.34	Explanation:

Stock Price Lesson Review

1. Explain how a stock price can decrease or increase in value.
   _____
   _____
   _____
   _____
   _____

2. Which of the following is a ticker symbol? Select <u>ALL</u> that apply.
   a. McDonald's
   b. MCD
   c. Nike
   d. NKE

3. How do you know if a company's stock price has dropped?
   _____
   _____
   _____
   _____
   _____

Bull Market vs. Bear Market Pre-Lesson KWL Chart

The K-W-L chart helps you to think about your personal learning goals before you begin a lesson. What do you already know about the terms "bull market" and "bear market?" What do you want to know? After the lesson is completed, come back to this chart and reflect on what you have learned.

Complete the chart by listing what you know, want to know, and have learned (after the lesson) about the bull and bear markets.
Know
Want to know
Learned

Bull Market vs Bear Market

Words That Matter
Find these words in the lesson!

bull market	when stock prices are rising or expected to rise
bear market	when stock prices are falling or expected to fall
analogy	a comparison between two things

COMMON CORE STATE STANDARDS
- CCRA.L.2 - Demonstrate command of the conventions of standard English capitalization, punctuation, and spelling when writing.
- CCSS.ELA-LITERACY.W.4.4-W.6.4 - Produce clear and coherent writing in which the development and organization are appropriate to task, purpose, and audience.

LEARNING GOAL:
Students will be able to explain the difference between a bull market and bear market.

? Question to Ponder:

Why are bulls and bears used an analogy for the stock market?
_____
_____
_____
_____

🔍 Let's Explore the Topic:

These terms are not actually about bulls and bears. It's an **analogy** used to describe changes in the stock market. When investors talk about the **bull market**, they mean that stock prices are rising. The market is being compared to a bull raising its horns upward during an attack. In the **bear market**, stock prices are going down like a bear attacking its prey.

Black Millionaires of Tomorrow

Digging Deeper: Bulls and Bears

Bulls and Bears

Read each scenario. Circle the bear if the scenario describes a bear market. Circle the bull if the scenario describes a bull market. Explain the reason for your answer below.

Janelle visits her stockbroker for investment advice. The stockbroker tells her that the market is good. Stock prices have increased by 20% and the demand for stock is high. She encourages Janelle to invest in the current market.	 This is a _____ market because: _____ _____ _____ _____
Damian wants to invest in stocks. He uses the internet to research the current market. Damian notices that several companies are losing money, and their stock prices have decreased. Damian is concerned because he does not want to invest while the market is bad. He does not want to lose money.	 This is a _____ market because: _____ _____ _____ _____
Antoine is thinking about buying stock in black-owned clothing companies. He selects 3 companies and checks their stock prices daily for 1 week. Antoine notices a steady increase in the companies' stock prices. He decides to go ahead and invest.	 This is a _____ market because: _____ _____ _____ _____

Bulls and Bears Lesson Review

1. What is the economic difference between a bull market and a bear market?
   _____
   _____
   _____
   _____
   _____

2. The term "bull market" is used when _____.
   a) Stock prices are going down
   b) Stock prices are going up
   c) The price of bulls is going up
   d) Nobody is buying stocks

3. How are animal characteristics used to describe changes in the stock market?
   _____
   _____
   _____
   _____
   _____

Dividends Pre-Lesson KWL Chart

The K-W-L chart helps you to think about your personal learning goals before you begin a lesson. What do you already know about dividends? What do you want to know? After the lesson is completed, come back to this chart and reflect on what you have learned.

Complete the chart by listing what you know, want to know, and have learned (after the lesson) about dividends.
Know
Want to know
Learned

Dividends

Words That Matter
Find these words in the lesson!

| dividend | a portion of a company's earnings that is given to its shareholders |

COMMON CORE STATE STANDARDS
- CCRA.L.2
  Demonstrate command of the conventions of standard English capitalization, punctuation, and spelling when writing.
- CCSS.ELA-LITERACY.W.4.4-W.6.4
  Produce clear and coherent writing in which the development and organization are appropriate to task, purpose, and audience.
- CCSS.MATH.CONTENT.4.NBT.B.4 & 5
  Fluently add, subtract and multiply multi-digit whole numbers using the standard algorithm

LEARNING GOAL:
Students will be able to explain and calculate dividends.

Question to Ponder:

Why do companies offer dividends to their shareholders?
_____
_____
_____
_____

Let's Explore the Topic:

Some companies pay **dividends** to their shareholders. This is an extra benefit of investing in a company's stock. When companies offer dividends, they can attract more investors. Some companies are financially successful and can afford to pay out dividends, while others cannot.

Dividends can be paid in the form of cash, shares or property. The amount of a dividend usually depends on how many shares you own. Dividends can be paid monthly or quarterly (4 times per year). Once you get your dividends, you can be a consumer or an investor. That means that you can either spend it or re-invest it.

Extension Activity

Look at the Dividend Calendar at https://www.nasdaq.com/dividend-stocks/dividend-calendar.aspx How is this information helpful for investors? Which companies currently offer the best dividends?

Digging Deeper: Dividends

Calculate the Dividends

Read the scenarios and use mathematics to calculate the dividends.

Example: Carl owns 45 shares in the company, PepsiCo. This month, he will receive a dividend payment of $0.92 per share. How much money will Carl receive?

$$45 \text{ shares} \times \$0.92 = \$41.40$$

Carl will receive a monthly dividend payment of $41.40

Kenyatta owns 120 shares in the company, Walmart. She receives quarterly dividend payments. If Walmart pays out $1.13 per share, how much money will Kenyatta receive within 1 year?

Nick owns 74 shares in the company, Adidas. If he receives monthly dividend payments at $1.55 per share, how much money will he receive in 6 months?

Leona owns 41 shares in a local restaurant chain. She received a monthly dividend payment of $50.84. How much is the dividend payment per share?

23

Dividend Lesson Review

1. Why do some companies offer dividends, while others do not?
   _____
   _____
   _____
   _____
   _____

2. If you earned dividends from an investment, what would you do with the money?
   _____
   _____
   _____
   _____
   _____

Mutual Funds Pre-Lesson KWL Chart

The K-W-L chart helps you to think about your personal learning goals before you begin a lesson. What do you already know about mutual funds? What do you want to know? After the lesson is completed, come back to this chart and reflect on what you have learned.

Complete the chart by listing what you know, want to know, and have learned (after the lesson) about mutual funds.

Know
Want to know
Learned

Mutual Funds

Words That Matter
Find these words in the lesson!

mutual fund	an investment type that includes multiple investors and/or investments
diversification	investing in multiple types of investments
investment club	a group of members who invest and manage their own money

COMMON CORE STATE STANDARDS
- CCRA.L.2 - Demonstrate command of the conventions of standard English capitalization, punctuation, and spelling when writing.
- CCSS.ELA-LITERACY.W.4.4-W.6.4 - Produce clear and coherent writing in which the development and organization are appropriate to task, purpose, and audience.
- CCSS.MATH.CONTENT.6.RP.A.3.C - Find a percent of a quantity as a rate per 100
- CCSS.MATH.CONTENT.5.NF.B.3 - Solve word problems involving division of whole numbers leading to answers in the form of fractions or mixed numbers
- CCSS.MATH.CONTENT.4.OA.A.3 - Solve multistep word problems posed with whole numbers and having whole-number answers using the four operations

LEARNING GOAL:
Students will be able to explain the benefits of investing in a mutual fund.

❓ Question to Ponder:

You and a friend are thinking about combining your money so that you can invest together. Is this a good idea? Why or why not?

___
___
___
___

Let's Explore the Topic:

Mutual funds can be beneficial because they offer **diversification**. It's like the old saying, "don't put all your eggs in one basket." Instead of buying stock in one company, you can spread out your money and invest in different companies. If one company loses money, your other investments can remain safe.

Also, you can create a "money pool" with other investors. Imagine if you wanted to buy a pizza, but you didn't have enough money. So you and 3 other friends each contribute $5 to buy a pizza. This is the same concept of a mutual fund. Investors put their money together and invest in one or more companies. Sometimes, they form an **investment club** so that they can manage their own investments. But investment clubs have more rules, and members must meet and agree on financial decisions.

 ## Digging Deeper: Mutual Funds

The Mutual Fund

Read each scenario and use mathematics to calculate the answer.

Example: 4 people invested a total of $10,000 into a stock mutual fund. If each investor contributed an equal amount, how much did each person invest?

$$\$10{,}000 \div 4 = \$2{,}500$$

Each investor contributed $2,500.

David and Terrance invested in a $7,100 stock mutual fund. David contributed 40% of the total amount, while Terrance funded the rest. How much did each investor pay?

Shonda and 5 friends invested in a $35,000 stock mutual fund. If each person contributed the same amount, how much did each person invest? What fraction of the total amount did each person contribute?

Shavonne, Alicia and Kiara started an investment club. They pooled together a total of $60,000. Shavonne contributed 50% of the total investment. Alicia invested $10,000. How much did Kiara invest?

Mutual Funds Lesson Review

1. What are some of the benefits of mutual funds?
   _____
   _____
   _____
   _____
   _____

2. Mutual funds can help investors diversify because _____. Select **ALL** that apply.
   a) They offer multiple investment options
   b) They only offer one investment option
   c) The can include multiple investors

3. How can investing with other people be helpful?
   _____
   _____
   _____
   _____

Stock Market Myths Pre-Lesson KWL Chart

The K-W-L chart helps you to think about your personal learning goals before you begin a lesson. What do you already know about stock market myths? What do you want to know? After the lesson is completed, come back to this chart and reflect on what you have learned.

Complete the chart by listing what you know, want to know, and have learned (after the lesson) about stock market myths.
Know
Want to know
Learned

Black Millionaires of Tomorrow

Stock Market Myths

Words That Matter
Find these words in the lesson!

| myth | something that is commonly believed, but is not true |

COMMON CORE STATE STANDARDS
- CCRA.L.2 - Demonstrate command of the conventions of standard English capitalization, punctuation, and spelling when writing.
- CCSS.ELA-LITERACY.W.4.4-W.6.4 - Produce clear and coherent writing in which the development and organization are appropriate to task, purpose, and audience.

LEARNING GOAL:
Students will be able to identify at least 5 myths about the stock market.

❓ Question to Ponder:

How can myths keep people from investing in stocks?
_____
_____
_____
_____

🔍 Let's Explore the Topic:

Now that you know all about stocks, it's important that you understand a few things about investing. There are lots of **myths** that cause people to make bad investments or avoid investing altogether. Here are the most common myths about stock investments:
- **If a stock is or has done well, it will always do well.** Remember that stock value changes all the time.
- **Rich companies are the best companies to invest in.** This is not always true. Smaller companies can also offer good investments. Remember that sometimes small companies grow.

28

- **You should sell your stock if the market goes down.** As an investor, you have to be patient and consistent. You don't want to keep changing your mind about an investment. Remember that the market will eventually go back up.
- **You will always make money. That is not true.** You may lose money sometimes. Remember that investments come with risks.
- **If a company is doing well, you should invest all of your money into it.** It may seem like a good idea to put all of your money into a successful business. But remember that it is best to diversify your investments.

Digging Deeper: Don't Believe the Myths

Truth or Myth?

Look at each statement and decide whether or not it is true.

Example:

Statement: Only wealthy people should invest in mutual funds.

Truth or Myth? <u>Myth</u>

Explanation: Mutual funds are also a good option for people who do not have lots of money. They can create a "money pool" with other investors.

Statement #1: There are only a few stock exchanges located around the world.

Truth or Myth? _____

Explanation:

Statement #2: Some companies offer shareholder dividends, while others do not.

Truth or Myth? _____

Explanation:

Statement #3: The stock market can be dangerous because companies can easily lie and steal money.

Truth or Myth? _____

Explanation:

Statement #4: Stockbrokers are intermediaries who can access the stock market for you.

Truth or Myth? _____

Explanation:

Statement #5: A stock is a portion of a company's ownership, also known as a share.

Truth or Myth? _____

Explanation:

Stock Market Myths Lesson Review

1. Why is it important to debunk (or prove to be untrue) myths about investing in stocks?

2. Based on what you have learned, do you plan to invest in stocks? Why or why not?

Black Millionaires of Tomorrow Answer Key
Grades 4-6

Stocks Lesson

Question to Ponder: Answers will vary. A possible rationale for this answer is that companies sell stock in order to make more money.

Digging Deeper:

> **Investor 1:** Jaheim wants to purchase 50 shares priced at $16.08 each. Calculate the total cost of Jaheim's investment.
>
> 50 × $16.08 = $804
> Jaheim invested a total of $804.
>
> **Investor 2:** Brandy wants to purchase 75 shares priced at $16.08 each. Calculate the total cost of Brandy's investment.
>
> 75 × $16.08 = $1,206
> Brandy invested a total of $1,206.
>
> **Investor 3:** Vincent wants to purchase 120 shares priced at $16.08 each. He plans to later sell ¾ of his stocks at a higher price. Calculate the total cost of Vincent's investment. How many shares does he plan to sell?
>
> 120 × $16.08 = $1,929.60
> Vincent invested a total of $1, 929.60

Lesson Review:

1. Answers will vary. A possible rationale is that companies offer partial ownership in order to attract investors.

2. C A shareholder is a person who owns stocks.

3. Answers will vary. Students should be able to identify a company that they would like to invest in, and explain the reasons why.

Stock Market Lesson

Question to Ponder: Answers will vary. Students should be able to brainstorm some ideas about the stock market and its function.

Digging Deeper:
Students should be able to produce clear writing that addresses the task. Students should also use information from the chart to explain their reasoning.

Lesson Review:

1. One way to buy stock is through the online market. Students can list other ways to buy stock, as well.

2. b) The stock market is a physical or virtual market where people buy stocks.

Stockbroker Lesson

Question to ponder: Answers will vary. A possible rationale for this answer is that stockbrokers help investors buy stock.

Digging Deeper:

> **Mr. Gardner's broker fee is 2% of your total investments. You purchase 100 shares at $163.22 each. How much money will you owe Mr. Gardner for his services?**
>
> $100 \times \$163.22 = \$16{,}322$
>
> $\$16{,}322 \times 0.02 = \$326.44$
>
> You will have to pay Mr. Gardner a broker fee in the amount of $326.44.
>
> ---
>
> **A local competitor, Jada Morris, offers her brokerage services for $6.95 per trade (or per share purchase). If you conduct the same deal as the scenario above, whose services will cost you more? Mr. Gardner or Mrs. Morris?**
>
> $100 \times \$6.95 = \$695.00$
>
> Mrs. Morris' broker fee is higher than Mr. Gardner's.

Lesson Review:

1. A stockbroker is an intermediary who helps investors buy/sell stocks through the stock market.

2. d) All of these terms describe a stockbroker's role.

3. Answers will vary. A possible rationale for this answer is that stockbrokers offer a service in exchange for money.

Stock Exchange

Question to ponder: Answers will vary. Students should demonstrate an understanding of how the stock exchange connects investors and companies all over the world.

Digging Deeper:

> **Mario wants to purchase stock in Maple Leaf Manufacturing, a company based in Canada. Which stock exchange would this company be listed on?**
>
> This company would be listed on the TMX Group, which is based in Canada.
>
> **LaToya wants to purchase stock in Beauté Noire Cosmetics, a company based in Paris, France. Which stock exchange would this company be listed on?**
>
> This company would be listed on Euronext. Euronext is based in multiple locations, including Paris, France.
>
> **Ronnie wants to purchase stock in Nintendo, a company based in Japan. Which stock exchange would this company be listed on?**
>
> This company would be listed on the Japan Exchange Group, which is based in Tokyo, Japan.
>
> **Taj wants to purchase stock in Rajesh Exports, a company based in India. Which stock exchange would this company be listed on?**
>
> This company would be listed on the National Stock Exchange of India, which is based in Mumbai.
>
> **Mario wants to purchase stock in Mattel, a company based in California. Which stock exchange (or exchanges) would this company be listed on?**
>
> This company would be listed on the NYSE or NASDAQ, which are based in the United States (New York).

Lesson Review:

1. Answers will vary. Students should demonstrate an understanding of how the stock exchange connects investors and companies all over the world.

2. ⓑ, ⓒ, ⓔ These statements are true.

Stock Prices Lesson

Question to Ponder: Answers will vary. A possible rationale is that changes in the stock market can cause stock prices to rise and fall.

Digging Deeper:

Apple Inc AAPL ▼ - 2.41	**Explanation:** Apple's stock prices have decreased. The arrow is pointing downward, and the negative red number indicates a price drop.
Sony Corp SNE ▼ - 0.90	**Explanation:** Sony's stock prices have decreased. The arrow is pointing downward, and the negative red number indicates a price drop.
Walt Disney Co DIS ▲ + 0.34	**Explanation:** Disney's stock prices have increased. The arrow is pointing upward, and the positive green number indicates a price rise.

Lesson Review:

1. Stock prices change based on factors such as the economy and supply/demand.
2. ⓑ ⓓ MCD and NKE are both ticker symbols.
3. Stock price changes are indicated by the arrow direction and/or the color of the text. A downward arrow and red text indicates a price drop.

Bull Market vs. Bear Market Lesson

Question to Ponder: Answers will vary. Students should be able to explain how and why these animals are compared to changes in the stock market.

Digging Deeper:

Janelle visits her stockbroker for investment advice. The stockbroker tells her that the market is good. Stock prices have increased by 20% and the demand for stock is high. She encourages Janelle to invest in the current market.

This is a <u>bull</u> market because: <u>stock prices are going up.</u>

Black Millionaires of Tomorrow

Damian wants to invest in stocks. He uses the internet to research the current market. Damian notices that several companies are losing money, and their stock prices have decreased. Damian is concerned because he does not want to invest while the market is bad. He does not want to lose money.

This is a **bear** market because: stock prices are going down.

Antoine is thinking about buying stock in black-owned clothing companies. He selects 3 companies and checks their stock prices daily for 1 week. Antoine notices a steady increase in the companies' stock prices. He decides to go ahead and invest.

This is a **bull** market because: stock prices are going up.

Lesson Review:

1. In the bull market, the economy is doing well and stock prices are rising. In the bear market, the economy is not doing well and stock prices are dropping.

2. ⓑ The term "bull market" is used when stock prices are going up.

3. The bull market is being compared to a bull raising its horns upward during an attack. In the bear market, stock prices are going down like a bear attacking its prey.

Dividends Lesson

Question to ponder: Answers will vary. A possible rationale is that companies offer dividends in order to attract more investors.

Digging Deeper:

Kenyatta owns 120 shares in the company, Walmart. She receives quarterly dividend payments. If Walmart pays out $1.00 per share yearly, how much money will Kenyatta receive every quarter (4 payments per year)?

$$120 \times \$1.00 = \$120$$
$$\$120 \div 4 = \$30$$

Kenyatta will receive a $30 dividend payment every quarter.

> **Nick owns 74 shares in the company, Adidas. If he receives monthly dividend payments at $1.55 per share, how much money will he receive in 6 months?**
>
> $$74 \times \$1.55 = \$114.70$$
> $$\$114.70 \times 6 = \$688.20$$
>
> Nick will receive a total of $688.20 in dividend payments after 6 months.
>
> ---
>
> **Leona owns 41 shares in a local restaurant chain. She received a monthly dividend payment of $50.84. How much is the dividend payment per share?**
>
> $$\$50.84 \div 41 = \$1.24$$
>
> The restaurant chain pays out $1.24 per share.

Lesson Review:

1. Some companies can afford to pay out dividends, while others may need to keep the money for their business.

2. Answers will vary.

Mutual Funds Lesson

Question to ponder: Answers will vary. Students should be able to explain why they think that investing with a friend is a good/bad idea.

Digging Deeper:

> **David and Terrance invested in a $7,100 stock mutual fund. David contributed 40% of the total amount, while Terrance funded the rest. How much did each investor pay?**
>
> $$\$7,100 \times 0.40 = \$2,840$$
> $$\$7,100 - \$2,840 = \$4,260$$
>
> David invested $2,840. Terrance invested $4,260.
>
> ---
>
> **Shonda and 5 friends invested in a $35,000 stock mutual fund. If each person contributed the same amount, how much did each person invest? What fraction of the total amount did each person contribute?**
>
> $$\$35,000 \div 5 = \$7,000$$
>
> Each person invested $7,000. Each investor contributed 1/5 of the total amount.
>
> ---
>
> **Shavonne, Alicia and Kiara started an investment club. They pooled together a total of $60,000. Shavonne contributed 50% of the total investment. Alicia invested $10,000. How much did Kiara invest?**
>
> $$\$60,000 \times 0.50 \text{ or } \$60,000 \div 2 = \$30,000$$
> $$\$30,000 - \$10,000 = \$20,000$$
>
> Shavonne invested $30,000. Kiara invested $20,000.

Lesson Review:

1. Answers will vary. A possible rationale is that mutual funds allow investors to diversify.

2. ⓐ, ⓒ Mutual funds offer multiple investment options and can include multiple investors.

3. Answers will vary. A possible rationale is that investors can combine their money in order make larger investments.

Stock Market Myths Lesson

Question to ponder: Answers will vary. A possible rationale for this answer is that people may not want to invest based on a negative idea or belief.

Digging Deeper:

Statement #1: There are only a few stock exchanges located around the world.
Truth or Myth? Myth
Explanation: There are many stock exchanges located around the world.

Statement #2: Some companies offer shareholder dividends, while others do not.
Truth or Myth? Truth
Explanation: Some companies cannot afford dividend payments. You will not always receive dividend payments when you invest in stock.

Statement #3: The stock market can be dangerous because companies can easily lie and steal money.
Truth or Myth? Myth
Explanation: The stock market is regulated by the SEC in order to prevent fraud and theft.

Statement #4: Stockbrokers are intermediaries who can access the stock market for you.
Truth or Myth? Truth
Explanation: The stock market is not public like a store. You need an intermediary, such as a stockbroker, in order to buy stock.

Statement #5: A stock is a portion of a company's ownership, also known as a share.
Truth or Myth? Truth
Explanation: A share is portion of a company's ownership.

About the Author

Dr. Boyce D. Watkins is one of the leading financial scholars and social commentators in America. He advocates for education, economic empowerment and social justice and has changed the definition of what it means to be a Black scholar and leader in America.

He is one of the founding fathers of the field of Financial Activism which has the objective of creating social change through the use of conscientious capitalism. He is a Blue Ribbon Speaker with Great Black Speakers, Inc. and one of the most highly sought after public figures in the country.

In addition to publishing a multitude of scholarly articles on finance, education and black social commentary, Dr. Watkins has presented his message to millions, making regular appearances in various national media outlets, including CNN, Good Morning America, MSNBC, FOX News, BET, NPR, *Essence Magazine*, *USA Today*, The Today Show, ESPN, The Tom Joyner Morning Show and CBS Sports.

Educationally, Dr. Watkins earned BA and BS degrees with a triple major in Finance, Economics and Business Management. In college, he was selected by the Wall Street Journal as the Outstanding Graduating Senior in Finance. He then earned a Master's Degree in Mathematical Statistics from University of Kentucky and a Ph.D. in Finance from Ohio State University and was the only African-American in the world to earn a PHD in Finance during the year 2002. He is the founder of The Black Wealth Bootcamp, The Black Business School and The Your Black World coalition, which have a collective total of 300,000 subscribers and 1.4 million social media followers world-wide.

In 2017, Simmons College, an HBCU in Kentucky, announced the creation of The Dr. Boyce Watkins Economic Empowerment Institute, where the goal is to develop black economic leaders for the 21st century and beyond.

Dr. Watkins is also the founder of The Black Business School and The Black Wealth Bootcamp, which have over 50,000 students.

Made in the USA
Columbia, SC
20 May 2020